Our Lady of Perpetual Desert

POEMS by

ALEXANDRA MARTINEZ

AN INLANDIA INSTITUTE PUBLICATION

RIVERSIDE, CALIFORNIA

ISBN: 978-1-955969-15-4

Book design and layout: Mark Givens
Printed and bound in the United States
Distributed by Ingram

Library of Congress Cataloging-in-Publication Data

Names: Martinez, Alexandra, 1991- author.
Title: Our lady of the perpetual desert : poems / by Alexandra Martinez.
Description: First edition. | Riverside, California : Inlandia Institute,
  [2023]
Identifiers: LCCN 2022052117 | ISBN 9781955969154 (paperback)
Subjects: LCGFT: Poetry.
Classification: LCC PS3613.A786387 O97 2023 | DDC 811.6--dc23/eng/20221031
LC record available at https://lccn.loc.gov/2022052117

Published by Inlandia Institute
Riverside, California
www.InlandiaInstitute.org
First Edition

Our Lady of Perpetual Desert

POEMS by

ALEXANDRA MARTINEZ

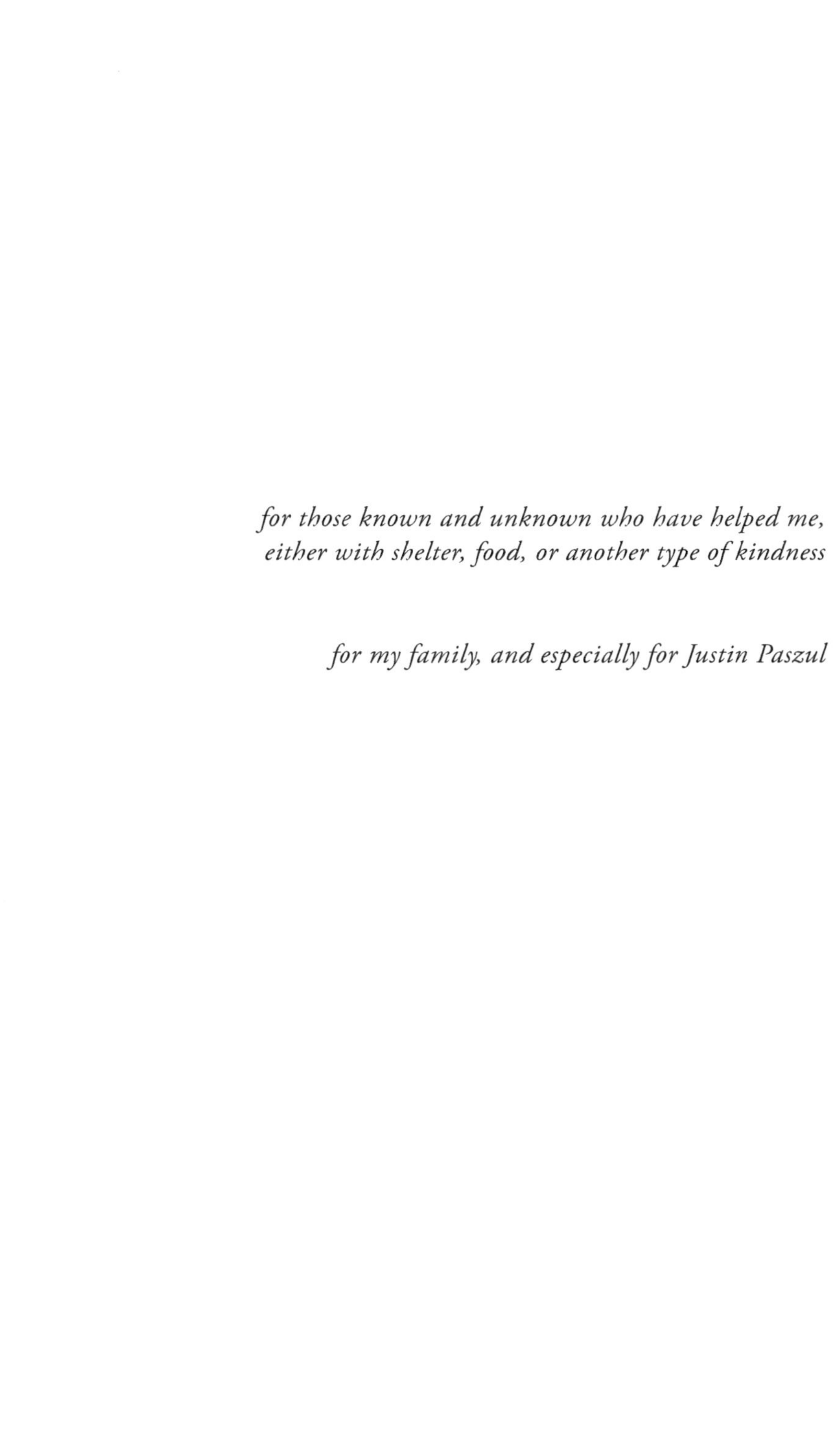

*for those known and unknown who have helped me,
either with shelter, food, or another type of kindness*

for my family, and especially for Justin Paszul

*Sincere gratitude to the editors of the following publications
in which some of these poems first appeared:*

WAX NINE
  (*California, California Condor, Absolutely Curtains*)

RESURRECTION MAG
  (*Fuck the Clock*)

SOBOTKA LIT MAG
  (*Peace Pilgrim*)

ANOTHER NEW CALLIGRAPHY
  (*Citrus Again, After my grandfather got a new pacemaker*)

SOOTH SWARM JOURNAL
  (*America*)

COSMONAUTS AVENUE
  (*Citrus is my only home*)

VAGABOND CITY LIT
  (*Citrus*)

CUTTHROAT; A JOURNAL OF THE ARTS
  (*Brother Rabbit, Homeland Security, All of my father's friends*)

DRYLAND
  (*Somewhere, Ocean*)

NO TENDER FENCES
  (*Quake*)

CONTENTS

I

Conroe, Texas

"Everybody I know seems to know me well,
but does anybody know I'm gonna move like hell?"
— What Is and What Should Never Be, Led Zeppelin

In middle school, Bree and I used to walk the deer path and smoke cigarettes on our way to the basketball court in the new housing development our families had moved to. The only difference between housing complexes and housing developments is money. Bree's family had money, my family had strategic impulses at best. One day, Bree brought me her dad's copy of Led Zeppelin's BBC Sessions box set. She said, *be careful with this, man, if my dad knew I was sharing it with a Mexican he would kill me.* I wondered if her dad knew about the cigarettes.

I went home and listened and every song reminded me of Bree. Earlier she had said she had sex with some boy and was maybe pregnant but that she had thrown herself down the stairs and her sister had punched her in the stomach for good measure but maybe tomorrow after school we could take the bus to the clinic maybe?

Citrus Is My Only Home

To bite into an orange is not the same as to cut
into an orange is not the same
as to pick the orange

Ask my father, he knows the difference.

He buys a five pound bag from the same man by the overpass
once a week,
sometimes twice. My sister and I beg him to stop. We have too
many oranges in the house and
some of them are starting to mold and smell: sickly, sweet decay.

But no, today oranges, tomorrow cherries.

his uncles
had to eat wet dog food while working the fields

"They put it on the stove and wrapped it up in a tortilla!
Can you believe that shit?"

He says,

Laugh:

to keep from crying

that's why he buys all these oranges to feed us
Rotten fruit
instead of
dog food

One summer all my mom would eat were pepitas
she'd buy in five pound bags from the señoras at the swap meet

My sister and I rolled our eyes at the stench:
sweet rotting orange salty seeds all sweat and tears

Now we squeeze oranges over our heads
Let their yolks drip down
And take turns
Baptizing each other in the sea

Citrus

When I was a girl I ate whole oranges
The taste of sweet pulp and bitter peel
like eating sunlight
Before me there was Abuelo
Picking grapes
Before me there was Pa
Picking oranges
He must have laughed as he saw me
The fruit of his labors in my mouth

PEACE PILGRIM
for Rebecca Solnit

For centuries
people have been doing the long walk,
the pilgrimage.
Even when they didn't know they were
their feet, their soles, their bodies all said:

"This is right now a pilgrimage"
"This is right now a rite of passage"
"This is right now freedom"

The Peace Pilgrim knew this feeling.
She would walk for hours in peaceful contemplation,
she carried nothing and wanted nothing,
but received plenty.

For many,
pilgrimage is a god that promises health and wealth.
The pilgrims I know are red dirt and a lowrider spraypainted
in god's name.
They are asking to be free of diabetes and back pain and things
so simple that if I were a god I'd hand these to them from atop
my tufa throne
and say nothing but
"See you again next year."

The one time I felt like a pilgrim,
I stood outside a cathedral entrance in Mexico.
I crossed myself before getting down on my knees,
and joined the procession of people shuffling their bodies
forward on the worn marble floor.

The pain was immediate, the distance was long.
I tried to focus on what I wanted but did not know what it was.
I was young and could afford to learn more about pain.

We have all been dragging our knees across the broken sidewalks
of this place, collecting dirt, dust, and little pebbles in the craters
of our knees. When we reach our destination, we will cool
ourselves in the shade, point back at the trail we have made and
say,
"Is that enough?"

Mexican Piggy Bank

I used to have a mexican piggy bank. It was a black velveteen panther with cheap lead gold paint for eyes. Once, at a family party, my aunt asked me to show her where I kept it. I brought it out to her, but dropped it, and it shattered on the tile floor. My mother and father watched as she helped me clean the mess and we both picked up my collection of coins. They pretended not to notice when she slipped quarters into her pockets instead of my hands. This infuriated me. I stayed silent and stroked a velveteen shard I had put in my pocket.

Brother Rabbit

I have milked many bereaved moons
of questions I already know the answers to.
I have wondered in the desert
For my little brother who
never stood a chance here.

Look at me, a dry orange peel
Desiccated and afraid next to rabbit roadkill.
The crow that circles above is my sister's compass,
it screeches to her:
"They are here!
They are here!"

But my sister is too hunched
over to see
And too sleepy to hear
And too young
To care.

She hates parked cars
by the side of the road
She hates parked cars
by the side of the road
with one man as the driver.

I hate parked cars
by the side of the road
with men in them too.
We think the same thought
when we walk by them alone

We think
If my brother were here
If my brother were here
As we dig our nails into orange peel
Feel the skin and pulp crack
into our hands
Spit out seeds at parked cars
by the side of the road
My sister's compass screeches to my   roadkill body
I stopped walking a long time ago
Laid down next to rabbit
Called him my brother
And when she found us we'd been
tied together with a yoke of orange seeds.

Work Visa

My mom's name on a forged work visa:
Maria Mar
She was baptized this because
Mario is very easy to turn into Maria.
It means Mary of the Sea.

Years later there was a telenovela about a girl
with the same name.
It was one of those rags to riches tales.
I told my mom that in english her name meant,
     American Dream

She laughed and shook her head.

El Cometa

Once in Mexico we stopped at the end of a dirt road.
My father said:
the story goes, there was a little old man who
would ask for water at the end of this dirt road,
the story goes, this little old man was a ghost
if you stay quiet you can hear him rattling coins in a can.

My father was trying to scare us and it wasn't working until
he cut the lights from the car and I stood outside
and waved my hand in front of my face and could not see it.
In the quiet,
I listened for the little old man.
There was nothing.

I tasted dirt in my mouth and looked up
as a comet came blazing past.
It was so close it lit up the entire field in front of us.
My sister and I, we reached our arms
up in delight, and even now,
swear that we could touch it.

Silence

When I was 8 my father broke his wrist and couldn't work.
On the weekends he would wake me up early,
together we'd drive around the dumpsters of this town,
and collect cardboard.

Always cardboard, never cans. I don't know if he was being stubborn.
(He is very stubborn) or if the return on cardboard was higher then.
We'd spend the morning driving around in silence.

One morning, he found a dead man next to a dumpster.
That was the end of our work days together.
We both detest the smell of wet cardboard and wonder
the name of the dead man.

Thief

Along this avenue there's a portrait
on almost every glass window.

Not really a portrait but
a grainy still of surveillance camera footage.

Every portrait with the word

THIEF

scrawled on it.

Reminds me of the time,
entering a grocery store with my father,
we watched as a man ran in and grabbed
two boxes of diapers from a pyramid display.

My father took me by the hand and said
sometimes you have to do things
you don't want to in the name of family.

Indigo

Did you think
when we were 10 and 6,
kicking dirt around
the desert slopes where we'd say hello to
owls and jackrabbits and
wander through eucalyptus hair, pull it aside to peek
at the golf course

Did you think that they would put up a fence
and flatten out the weedy spines covering the ground
and did you think in those days
we spent
tugging eucalyptus leaves and licking them
and eating them and ignoring
our bellyaches by throwing golf balls
back through the tree forest

Did you think these days that we'd stand outside that
fence staring at all the nothingness that then was enough
and now was some developer's canvas
Did you think these days we wouldn't
even know each other's name?

Las Golondrinas

In the mountains we climbed up and then we scaled down.
There were birds all around us, little swallows. We ate
oranges, spitting out the seeds on every jagged stone step like
Buddhists counting beads between their fingers. Or maybe
like my mother sitting in a church pew. The birds were singing
and I was trying to decide whether I tasted citrus or blood.

According to my father we never swung from trees but he
said he saw a ghost hanging from one. He was a revolutionary
soldier, he said. He wasn't afraid then because he was young
but now he is old and tired and I can tell that he gets terrified
every time I ask him about the hanged man.

My mother and father go to church every Sunday, not together
but united in the Holy Spirit. My sister and I watch from a
pew and peel oranges, bored and wondering when god will
come find us because we've grown tired of looking for him.

II

Summer in Glendale, NY

Sitting on my back stoop listening
to the Stooges' Funhouse
for the second time in a row.
Eating pineapple caramel
ice cream in a waffle cone
from the Hawaiian
bakery on the
corner.

Wondering if the raccoon that
always harasses me when I'm
back here will make an appearance.

What's the point of
living so close to
Houdini's grave anyway?

The Blue Stove

When I peeled and pitted the peaches
my hands would become deep red and
cracked and bloody from where the peeler
would mistake my skin for the skin of the fruit.

When I peeled and pitted the peaches
we would talk about everything and
nothing to pass the hours of pain
through our hands and feet,
all numb.

We'd collect the peach juice in our
freezing sleeves and
drink the rum in the storage room for
warmth and entertainment.

We'd get closer to each other.

Cover each other in bandaids and hugs and
laughs and tears and
at the end we'd be surrounded by towers
of peaches peeled pitted and sliced.
The rum would talk and say,
wow we did all this today
and we'll do it again
tomorrow.

the girls in the kitchen meet up when the moon is still setting
then brew coffee//melt butter//talk shit//get to work//knead the
dough//stir the filling//confess every sin//devour every desire//
all the while//taste this//taste that//the girls in the kitchen smile
at the delivery guys//take their time signing their names//say I'm
clocking out for break//say have a good day//to everyone
who was sleeping when they were already in the kitchen//the girls
in the kitchen//leave the kitchen//empty//like the girls in the
kitchen//were never there

CENTO TO KEEP YOU ALIVE

borrowing from Marwa Helal, Werner Herzog, Nick Flynn,
Kaveh Akbar, Charles Bukowski, and Ada Limon

ONCE YOU BEGIN YOU WILL FIND THAT YOU
CAN NO LONGER AFFORD TO NOT FEEL. WALK
STRAIGHT AHEAD, NEVER DETOUR. THE RADIO
CLAIMS THE SECRET IS SIMPLE: YOU ALWAYS
NEED TO WANT TO KNOW WHAT COMES NEXT.
LET THAT PULL YOU BACK FROM THE LEDGE
AGAIN & AGAIN. SPEND THE YEAR DRINKING IN
THE DESERT. KNOW THAT YOU ARE UNENDING.

III

America

While you were asleep me and your dad sang all of American Pie
him in the front seat me in the back and it made me want to cry
because I wanted him to know how much I wanted to be what
he wanted me to be but all he says is bye bye miss American Pie
I wanted to tell him about the girl with skin browner than me
and how we'd drive around in her little blue scoot scoot with this
exact song playing loud and all the windows down to let winter
remind us that we were still walking along the edge of a levy of
the mind but all he said was bye bye miss American Pie and I am
trying to explain to him that there were plenty of us girls raised
on tortillas y los Beatles and that we love this goddamn country
eternally we love the frost on the pines and we love the desert
needles and we'd seen so much more of America than he would
ever see that we've been on all the highways and ran out of cars
screaming like banshees about how much we loved these stars but
I can't say any of this so instead I bake him the goddamn best
American Pie he eats it all and still says bye bye

Truth

The simple but awful truth:
I wasn't crying over seventeen dead but I was
Crying over the man who sat next to me on the train
Because his work boots were held together by duct tape.
He was carrying his tools and his head in his hands.

The working pour into neck/back/shoe breaking work

Somehow we're supposed to keep it all together
Cry over this/not that
Why not all of it?

Detention

In a Mexican rainforest there's a surreal castle
built by an eccentric Englishman. There
I stared at a tiger in a cage and felt nothing.
Then came across a small garter snake
and broke out into hives.

In Sedona I came across a tarantula but thought nothing.
And then I met you and I could smell the wet clay of that day.

There's a story my mother tells me whenever I meet a new man.
It's not a story about her,
I know she's many different women but
I never know which one I'm talking to.

She tells me of her cousin, The She-Wolf.
La Loba, she says.
When she first came to America, in Arizona we had
some relatives who took her in.
She says in the back room was La Loba.
Or her cousin Alma, who was cursed by
a man whose advances she rejected.

Alma was a teller at a bank and every week
the man arrived with gifts.
It didn't matter that she
had already said no once, twice,
three times.

So Alma reluctantly would walk home with

a teddy bear,
flowers, chocolates
in a heart shaped box.

It was the chocolates that did her in.
She bit the sweet and became unhinged.
Her nails and hair grew long and wild.
She'd run up and down her bedroom walls,
scraping her nails, the noise
keeping her parents awake.

They put bars on her bedroom window to keep her from escaping
and brought a priest to wash away her sins.
She just howled like a dog kept in a crate for too long.

When my mother first saw her, she tried to speak to her.
Alma only grunted and curled up in the light of her window.

When Alma escaped
the family searched for weeks
until they surrendered her to the desert.

I imagine her free from the man,
walking barefoot in red clay.
Past the detention center where a child
has lived out three years of life, passing time by
learning english sitting in her mother's lap.
Pointing at things in picture books
she's yet to touch:

A teddy bear,
flowers,
chocolates in a heart shaped box.

Somewhere

Outside the library
all the jobless are walking around
staying out of the shade,
out of the embrace of the
Santa Ana Winds.
It's 2 o'clock and the clocktower plays
"Somewhere" from West Side Story
There's the couple I always see
The man shuffles in front of the woman
as she pushes their home along.
They don't notice
all the painted ladies
swarming around and how they
flutter slowly like falling confetti
inside the Staples Center.
Slowly,
like a migration.
The couple
does a loop around the park
and starts another one.
Peace and quiet and open air
Butterflies know nothing
of walls and fences and borders.
I wish for the couple the luck of butterflies
Somehow, someday, somewhere.

The night it all fell apart
or came together
(depending on who you ask)

I walked straight down the avenue towards the city lights
I was alone except for the
tired taxi drivers
going around in circles
or walking past me on the way home
from the depot

In my cold dry hand I held a paper cup tightly
and sipped   and sipped
and sipped
to feel the color on my lips
for my eyes to become newly discovered planets
Waiting
        waiting   waiting
for something different … better
Knowing this night: a demarcation of the before and after

The more I walked the brighter the lights became
orbs leading the way
I weaved on, warm and confident on the sidewalk
between the men in their celebration suits
reeking of champagne
I tipped my little paper cup at them
but they laughed and pushed me away

The night it all fell apart a woman in a green dress held me
She brushed my hair like a mother and told me everything
would be okay

Like all those years ago when I would wake screaming,
and my vigilant and silent mother would help me get back to sleep
she would place an egg in a glass under my bed
in the morning it would be rotten with the stuff inside me

Jesus

I saw Jesus in a cluster of flowers,
I smelled him in the wettest of earth,
The driest of clay.
I saw him as the wall that was the barrier
between the homeless encampment and
the shooting range.

What a kingdom, what an empire
where this
exists.

California Condor

I saw a headline that read "the condors are back in California!"
and under that someone said,
"Great, just what 2020 needed!"

As if
the condors are the ones
stealing people's babies from their beds
creeping up behind young women on the streets and telling them,

Shhhhhh
All the power in the world is mine and because of that so are you

As if
the condors are the ones
stepping out of vehicles so self-assured that the only thing they
need to say is
stop!
and proceed to shoot bullets into a human body

This type of vulture will take a knee when a news camera is
around.
In every one of these videos the vulture turns and smiles and
everybody claps because it is
such a nice condor.
But there are other videos, we all know.

Tonight, we slept outside and looked at the stars.
We silently watched as
a giant bird shadowed in black
circled slowly overhead.
I prayed it was a real condor.

Quake

Quake rattles cages,
like teeth rattle in my head when
I count down backwards
in an attempt at sleep
that says,
"I'm not awake but I'm not dreaming either."
Like this one time
I dreamt
desert owls were pecking at my wrists
while my feet were bandaged in a flag of
an eagle capturing a snake.
Then there were too many snakes,
not enough owls.
Needed saint patrick or,
something holy.
instead we got this:
"Sometimes by losing a battle you find a new way to win the war."
How about we secede ourselves
into the ocean?
The walls of waves our only threat.
Waves that keep crashing closer,
shrinking the shoreline at my feet.
Salt on my tongue,
With my eyes bloodshot-sand
I look over the gold and purple horizon
at a wall.

Homeland Security

I saw you shake a canteen and then
empty it with glee.

The water melts away that desert where once, on
TV, I saw a reporter crack an egg on a rock.

The camera came back later and it had fried perfectly.
It made my tiny mouth water with awe and shame.

Now, you are the one who separates
the yolk from the white,

every desert morning and throws them
all back to the other side where they belong.

You fill both skies with the smell of rotten eggs, a hiss
of steam when their shells are dropped into clear, boiling water.

Fuck the Clock

Oh my god

Fuck time zones and fuck what hour or day it is
the question should always be
is the sun or moon up where you are?
the answer will always be
yes

An addendum: fuck the clock

Patti Smith wore it first,
look it up.
On Instagram she's always posting pictures of her handwriting
or coffee or the moon and
honestly?
Same

I am trying to find meaning after watching a video of air being
moved around,
that's putting it lightly,
of fire, of an explosion.
I am trying to find meaning after waking up
at the dark pre-sunrise hour and looking into the horizon and
seeing another fire burning here.

The fire there is unlike
the fire here but they are both the same
in that they remind me of chaos theory or more specifically the
butterfly effect.

Homero Gómez González, patron saint of butterflies was
murdered this year.
This year that has murdered so many

in a different time zone than mine.
In my time zone people create
native plant gardens for
butterflies to call home
or suburban lawns for
no one.

IV

Total Facts Known About Lou Reed

1. You get kicked out of class for not
   standing for a pledge
   or refusing to cross your heart.

2. You get kicked out of ROTC
   for threatening your commander with a gun.

   Later you say, *isn't that what they wanted?*

3. You spend decades practicing tai chi
   even though you quit karate after one day.
   The martial arts for you are
   a slow sweep across white sands landscape.

4. You are a Coney Island Baby when caught on
   a Rockaway wave in a bikini the color of a Warhol,
   screaming to the shore
   I'm set free!

5. You die in your garden with your
   legs steady and shoulder-width apart.
   Your arms held parallel to the soft wet grass,
   Your heart stopped when you were in the middle of
   creating a hummingbird.

6. You say:
   At last
   I'm beginning to see the light!

In the Morning He Feeds the Deer

for Byron Herbert Reece

I can still smell the chew
collecting in a 49ers cup in the cupholder of his Mustang
with its Sons of Confederate Veterans sticker on the bumper.

In the morning,
I would watch the fog collecting over the mountains.
Below us, I could walk to the mailing address for
the International Keystone Knights of the Ku Klux Klan.

Next to that was a meadow,
and in it a podium rising from the mist,
with the letters
K
  K
   K
all in red.

I would talk with your mother in the kitchen,
she would pour me coffee and hover over me as you slept.

When I told her what I liked to do, she told me about the poet
who was buried at a cemetery nearby.
He taught at the local college in the 50s.
Later, I would try to find his grave,
but couldn't.

Instead, you and I hike Blood Mountain,
where the poet was born.
I don't tell you that I had to escape your mother's house,
but I do tell you this is the worst Thanksgiving I've ever had.

You just stare through me while I say this, usually my
expectations are pretty low.
When we reach the peak I realize it feels good to crack sticks
under my boots
especially when all I hear is your parents saying: eee-lee-gulls

Stretched out loud in that perfect way that I hate.

Seated at the table, you watched as I put down the fork and raised
the knife.
You didn't say anything but begged me not to make a scene.
The whole time I sat in drunk silence and thought of the podium
and the meadow,
and how to set it all ablaze.

At the end of the night I walked past the portrait of the
confederate soldier.
He watched me with his stag blank eyes while I sat on the floral
bedspread
and read about the Blood Mountain poet who
grew up on a farm
got awards and recognition
was a laureate
and killed himself.

I never did find his grave,
but if I ever do, I'll lay down next to it and
place my hand and ear on the earth.

Nature Documentary

My father and I watch as the walruses
tumble into the rocks below.
We watch as they weightlessly
Take the unexpected
last dive of their lives.
My mother and I watch as the man
with the ponytail feeds the
wild parrots of San Francisco.
We watch with the passersby.
I notice a man stop and look like men do
when they're saying
I'm not impressed by this
I want to show him
What happens when all the ice melts;
when every floe is gone,
and every walrus dies.
Instead he walks away muttering
They're not really wild
They're not really wild

Sudan

Tell me in thousands of years
where it hurts
Tell me in grayscale
how it bruises

Give me your paw
Our moon cycles breathing in
and out of focus until I look up to see
the stars have pushed
your moon away

Here in the cool black dark
with no one else around
I hear a sound like the way
water drips into my bedroom
after a rain

Like the way it drips
from a leaf as you nuzzle it,
so peaceful
as if to say:
thank you I will only
take what I need

In thousands of years of being wrong
we keep perfecting it
I dip my index finger in white dust
I rubbed off this crumbling ceiling

It is damp and smells like my nosebleeds
I take it and mark my forehead like Ash Wednesday
My dust points at your moon

Can you smell the cool earth still?
Can you smell my iron?

On your moon there is no need for camouflage
there is no need for run
there is no bucket to catch the rain
or napkin to catch the blood
There is you: two black eyes and
ash mud resting gently in the shadow
of the crescent moon

Can you smell the cool earth still?

Sudan was the world's last male Northern White Rhino.

Poem for Ralph's Bodega on Lafayette Ave.

Holding kids hostage is an act of terrorism
said the spray painted bedsheet on the bodega awning

The year was 2018 and now
the year is 2020 and the kids are still
hostages and america is
still a terrorist

My body is falling apart and my mother's brain
has iron deposits
Only one of those things
is true

I can pretend to have no control
over my body but it is
still my body
Unlike my mother's brain
which is not mine

I used to think my mother was a fish
Now she seems more like the wind that grazes flowers and
shakes their scent into the air

My body is mine until
I am reminded by the lady at the DMV
that it's not when she says
Thank you for being a donor
Like she's waiting for me to hand her a shoulder
Or a spleen or whatever else is inside of me

I guess this isn't really a poem for a bodega
but it's for my mother and my body
And all the cages that I want to rip apart

Linda Ronstadt can't sing anymore.
A disease took her voice.
My mother can't remember her birthday
or what day it is
Or what she did yesterday.
A disease took her mind.

And yet,
every single day Linda sings to us.
And yet,
every single day my mother tells me how beautiful I am.

When Linda Ronstadt sings,
my mother's mind is awake and present.

Linda Ronstadt sings from *Canciones de mi Padre*,
Her voice frozen in time.
My mother sings along to every single line.

And every single night she says,
"We haven't watched Linda sing in a very long time."

Sometimes, during "Cancion Mixteca," my mother and I cry.
If I look closely enough, I see a tear roll down Linda's cheek too.

Garden Psalm

I plopped my mother in the garden and a tomato//in my mouth// we are homegrown//like terrorism//like the white lady on the podcast talking about how//she didn't realize how important//free time was until she found religion//what is my religion

A song started playing when I was writing this//the singer said// my friends my family they mean so much to me//I agree but remember that the singer beat his girlfriend//everything is like terrorism//last night there was another mass shooting//not like terrorism//but actually terrorism

If I keep saying that word will it lose its meaning//my mother sits in the garden// she loves the sun on her face// my mother can't remember her birthday// or the concept of terrrorism// everything is terrorism

After my grandfather got a new pacemaker

The nurse sang "Que Sera, Sera"
and we smiled at her as she took his blood pressure.
He had to stay an extra day because it was too high.
I look at his swollen feet sometimes, and want to rub them for him
because I think it would bring him comfort.
Sometimes I watch him when he falls asleep on the couch
and I take his arm to wake him and tell him to go to bed.
He never listens
and when the nurse sang "Que Sera, Sera"
he didn't hear that either.

V

Yessenia Zamudio

You like to tell me who I am
when you don't even like the sound of your own voice.

But the thing to remember is that
I am the hand that gently douses the back
of a cop's neck with gasoline.

I am the fingers that strike the match
that sets him ablaze and as he's
rolling around in his own melt
I am still moving like a wildfire.

This is when I become the spit that
comes out of Yessenia Zamudio's mouth
when she says:

**Yo no soy una colectiva/ni necesito un tambor/
ni necesito un pinche partido político que me represente/
yo me represento sola/y sin micrófono**

Her words are an incantation,
and I become a tumbleweed thousands of miles away.
Non-native and invasive, rejecting any existence
seen as useful to you or anyone.

Yo me represento sola

Citrus, Again

mold and softness
green, pliable like becoming
something else, like
like the
juice collecting under this tree
when the hungry ants
kiss each other around my
minor oasis my
legs tremble
watching them, thinking about you
my mouth is full of seeds
waiting to be spit
nowhere near you
or, maybe up that hill we frequent
where you tell me all the things you
plan us to be
my legs shake again considering these
quaint pictures of useful lives
how very good it must be,
to live that way

CALIFORNIA

The California Current System is a climate system that extends
from the Pacific
over the coast over the range over the grasslands over the sierras
It provides ~~moisture~~ life to 85% of the Redwood Forest floor
It is rapidly ~~disappearing~~ being disappeared

So far in 2019 I've seen a rosy boa in a rock outcropping
a rattlesnake in high, dry grass a garter snake in chaparral
a ball python wrapped around a girl's arm outside of Walmart

Ocean

In Puerto Rico there's a beach that's surrounded by a rock wall if you look at videos online you'll see there was a time where the ocean could crash over the rock wall and water would come in and fill into a half moon beach below but when I was there climate change had done away with that it was still possible to climb atop the black volcanic rock so I did that and all I could see was miles and miles of waves it felt colder up there and the wind was so strong that it was hard to stand up straight I made my way up higher on the sharp jagged rocks and watched a young boy stare out at the sea I could hear "Ocean" by the Velvet Underground playing in my head and felt that kind of rush you feel when you're exhilarated to be alive but also astounded at the easy opportunity to just end it all

Desert Star

A month ago my sister and I saw
An owl trailing upwards and across the
Plum skin black sky. We pointed like it was
A comet but you missed its calming drift.
Today driving in the dry toxic heat
Past the hospital we both saw a tall
Elegant feathered thing on the sidewalk.
A blue heron in this desert suburb,
We couldn't believe it as we drove by.
It made me forget that the tank was near
Empty and neither of us will get paid
This week. It made me forget the stench of
Smog and the road rage look in my rearview.

Money Tree

My money tree's leaves keep turning brown.
I pick them up from the dusty floor and put them in
my wallet for a rainy day.

Everybody in California has a swimming pool. I've counted them
all from a speeding train.
I've seen a boy with long dark hair skateboarding in an empty
one. It was too hot to go
outside and I was sick with one of those summer colds that
swallows your brain in its fist.
I watched the boy from a window as he made his way up one way
then down the other.
No dog paddles, no waves — just knees bent/hand touching
asphalt/all of him skimming the
hot air. Then splash! The blood: like water. The colors: like a
Hockney. I reached up and closed the blinds. Maybe tomorrow I
will go swimming.

Absolutely Curtains

when this is all over me and Gabrielle will sit in a booth at Dan Tana's
stir cocktails, practically dunk our hands in the icy alcohol
with greediness for belonging
the ancient bartender will be there even though he is now dead
Harry Dean Stanton will be there even though he's been dead
basically, everyone will be there whether dead or not
Dan Tana's will become the official in-between spot
The IT place it's always been
people will drive by and see nothing but shuttered windows,
know nothing of the joyous mess being made inside.

The Wasteland

Do people still think of the desert as a wasteland?
Saint Minerva certainly didn't.
I certainly don't either.

What is a wasteland anyway,
to people who think the desert is a wasteland?

In the desert, in maybe a foot, or three, or twenty
There are various life forms mingling
apart, but together
Growing
morphing
destroying

If you sit still long enough,
They'll let you join them.

What is a wasteland anyway?

Is it a long avenue of
warehouse
after warehouse
after warehouse
after warehouse
after warehouse
?

Lined with California native plants,
rows and rows of them.
Lined with sidewalks where no one
walks.

What is a wasteland?

Is it the 10
with amazon truck
after amazon truck
after amazon truck
?

I count them every day
on my way to work at 4 am.
I don't begrudge the drivers
because they're doing what I'm doing.
Exactly what we have to do,
to survive.

If the desert is a wasteland,
is that not a wasteland?

What is a wasteland anyway?

I've never gotten a delivery filled
with rock formations.
You could probably order some sort of
miniature of it.

You can definitely order some white sage.
You could probably order some native plants.
You could probably pick two-day shipping for all of these things.

But why would you, when the wasteland is right outside your door.

ABOUT ALEXANDRA MARTINEZ

Alexandra Martinez has been a nanny, dog walker, music writer, delivery person, sandwich artist, and baker among other things. She works for the San Bernardino County Library. She is a college dropout. Her essays, poetry, music reviews, and interviews have been published in various online and print outlets. She lives in the Inland Empire of Southern California.

ABOUT THE HILLARY GRAVENDYK PRIZE

The Hillary Gravendyk Prize is an open poetry book competition published by Inlandia Institute for all writers regardless of the number of previously published poetry collections.

HILLARY GRAVENDYK (1979-2014) was a beloved poet living and teaching in Southern California's "Inland Empire" region. She wrote the acclaimed poetry book, *HARM* from Omnidawn Publishing (2012) and the posthumoussly published *The Soluble Hour* (Omnidawn, 2017) and *Unlikely Conditions* (1913 Press, 2017, with Cynthia Arrieu-King) as well as the poetry chapbook *The Naturalist* (Anchiote Press, 2008). A native of Washington State, she was an admired Assistant Professor of English at Pomona College in Claremont, CA. Her poetry has appeared widely in journals such as *American Letters & Commentary, The Bellingham Review, The Colorado Review, The Eleventh Muse, Fourteen Hills, MARY, 1913: A Journal of Forms, Octopus Magazine, Tarpaulin Sky and Sugar House Review*. She was awarded a 2015 Pushcart Prize for her poem "Your Ghost," which appeared in the Pushcart Prize Anthology. She leaves behind many devoted colleagues, friends, family and beautiful poems. Hillary Gravendyk passed away on May 10, 2014 after a long illness. This contest has been established in her memory.

ABOUT INLANDIA INSTITUTE

Inlandia Institute is a regional non-profit and literary center. We seek to bring focus to the richness of the literary enterprise that has existed in this region for ages. The mission of the Inlandia Institute is to recognize, support, and expand literary activity in all of its forms in Inland Southern California by publishing books and sponsoring programs that deepen people's awareness, understanding, and appreciation of this unique, complex and creatively vibrant region.

The Institute publishes books, presents free public literary and cultural programming, provides in-school and after school enrichment programs for children and youth, holds free creative writing workshops for teens and adults, and boot camp intensives. In addition, every two years, the Inlandia Institute appoints a distinguished jury panel from outside of the region to name an Inlandia Literary Laureate who serves as an ambassador for the Inlandia Institute, promoting literature, creative literacy, and community. Laureates to date include Susan Straight (2010-2012), Gayle Brandeis (2012-2014), Juan Delgado (2014-2016), Nikia Chaney (2016-2018), and Rachelle Cruz (2018-2020).

To learn more about the Inlandia Institute, please visit our website at www.InlandiaInstitute.org.

OTHER HILLARY GRAVENDYK PRIZE BOOKS

How to Know You're Dreaming When You're Dreaming,
  Lesson One by Angelica Barraza
Winner of the 2021 National Hillary Gravendyk Prize

among the enemies by Michael Samra
Winner of the 2020 National Hillary Gravendyk Prize

This Side of the Fire by Jonathan Maule
Winner of the 2020 Regional Hillary Gravendyk Prize

The Silk the Moths Ignore by Bronwen Tate
Winner of the 2019 National Hillary Gravendyk Prize

Remyth: A Postmodern Ritual by Adam D. Martinez
Winner of the 2019 Regional Hillary Gravendyk Prize

All the Emergency-Type Structures by Elizabeth Cantwell
Winner of the 2018 Regional Hillary Gravendyk Prize

Our Bruises Kept Singing Purple by Malcolm Friend
Winner of the 2017 National Hillary Gravendyk Prize

Traces of a Fifth Column by Marco Maisto
Winner of the 2016 National Hillary Gravendyk Prize

God's Will for Monsters by Rachelle Cruz
Winner of the 2016 Regional Hillary Gravendyk Prize
Winner of a 2018 American Book Award

Map of an Onion by Kenji C. Liu
Winner of the 2015 National Hillary Gravendyk Prize

All Things Lose Thousands of Times by Angela Peñaredondo
Winner of the 2015 Regional Hillary Gravendyk Prize